FUN SONGS

Action
songs

Linda Mort

Check for CD
on Issue and Return

Credits

Author
Linda Mort

Text © Linda Mort 2005
© 2005 Scholastic Ltd

Editor
Jane Bishop

Designed using Adobe InDesign

Assistant Editor
Aileen Lalor

Published by Scholastic Ltd
Villiers House
Clarendon Avenue
Leamington Spa

Series Designer
Anna Oliwa

Warwickshire
CV32 5PR

Designer
Catherine Mason

www.scholastic.co.uk

Cover Illustration
Chris Simpson

Printed by Bell & Bain

2 3 4 5 6 7 8 9   5 6 7 8 9 0 1 2 3 4

Illustrations
Gaynor Berry

British Library Cataloguing-in-Publication Data
A catalogue record for this book is available from the British Library.

Music setting
Sally Scott

All songs supplied by CYP.

ISBN 0-439-97174-8
ISBN 978-0439-97174-4

Acknowledgement
Qualifications and Curriculum Authority for the use of extracts from the QCA/ DfEE document *Curriculum Guidance for the Foundation Stage* © 2000 Qualifications and Curriculum Authority.

Every effort has been made to trace copyright holders for the works reproduced in this book, and the publishers apologise for any inadvertent omissions.

Contents

Introduction 5

Myself

Tommy Thumb 6
Music 6
Lyrics 7
Activities 8
Photocopiable 9

Open, Shut Them 10
Music 10
Lyrics 11
Activities 12
Photocopiable 13

One Finger, One Thumb 14
Music 14
Lyrics 15
Activities 16
Photocopiable 17

At home

Polly, Put the Kettle On 18
Music 18
Lyrics 19
Activities 20
Photocopiable 21

Pat-a-cake, Pat-a-cake 22
Music 22
Lyrics 23
Activities 24
Photocopiable 25

Teddy Bear, Teddy Bear 26
Music 26
Lyrics 27
Activities 28
Photocopiable 29

Let's move!

The Grand Old Duke of York .. 30
Music 30
Lyrics 31
Activities 32
Photocopiable 33

Contents

Row, Row, Row Your Boat.......34

Music.......................................34
Lyrics.....................................35
Activities................................36
Photocopiable.........................37

Wind Your Bobbin Up...............38

Music.......................................38
Lyrics.....................................40
Activities................................42
Photocopiable.........................44

Musical fun

Here We Go Round the Mulberry Bush 42

Music.......................................42
Lyrics.....................................43
Activities................................44
Photocopiable.........................45

There Was a Princess Long Ago 46

Music.......................................46
Lyrics.....................................47
Activities................................48
Photocopiable.........................49

I am the Music Man.................50

Music.......................................50
Lyrics.....................................51
Activities................................52
Photocopiable.........................53

Animal fun

Incy Wincy Spider 54

Music.......................................54
Lyrics.....................................55
Activities................................56
Photocopiable.........................57

We're Going on a Bear Hunt.58

Music.......................................58
Lyrics.....................................59
Activities................................60
Photocopiable.........................61

Five Little Monkeys 62

Music.......................................62
Lyrics.....................................63
Activities................................64

Introduction

Using songs for learning

Music, songs and rhymes provide a natural means of active learning for young children. Many rhymes and songs help children to deal with worries and fears, for example about 'frightening' bears, and also provide opportunities for them to develop social skills such as taking turns.

Using songs, children can have fun with language, as they experiment with rhyme and alliteration, while they develop their vocabulary. By writing out the words to rhymes and songs on large sheets of paper, they can be used for shared reading with the children. Finger and action rhymes can also develop understanding of mathematical concepts such as counting one at a time, addition and subtraction.

Both modern and traditional rhymes, and songs about natural and manufactured phenomena, can develop the children's understanding of the world, both present and past. Physically, songs and rhymes enable young children to explore spatial concepts such as direction, and also to develop hand/eye coordination. All rhymes, songs and musical games provide a range of opportunities for the development of creative role-play, imagination and fantasy.

How to use this book

This book offers suggestions for imaginative activities to support the 15 lively action songs on the accompanying CD.

For each song, there are four pages. The first two consist of the song's musical arrangement, and the song words with suggested actions. The music enables practitioners to play the tunes themselves, introducing suitable percussion accompaniment. The second two pages consist of two sections headed 'Sharing the song' and 'Activity ideas', and a photocopiable activity for all the songs, except the last one.

'Sharing the song' explains the learning concepts which can be developed through the song, with suggested themes, appropriate times for singing the song, and ideas for introducing it. 'Activity ideas' suggests activities to follow up the song's concepts and themes. Each song is linked to a Stepping Stone and an Early Learning Goal. Collectively, the activity ideas cover all six Areas of Learning of the Foundation Stage (see box, below, for shorthand used).

Using the CD

Introduce each song by playing the CD, several times if possible, inviting the children to join in with the words while they copy your actions. Occasionally, use a glove puppet to act out the songs or sometimes play a song quietly in the background as the children are engaged in an activity related to the song. Many activities can take place outside, using a CD player in battery mode. This will also be a good opportunity for children to learn how to use the CD player independently. Demonstrate how to use it safely so that the children can operate it themselves. It will also be useful to provide a range of percussion instruments so that the children can accompany the songs. Additionally, create 'rhyme prop boxes' that relate to each song. Children can then use props in performance.

Areas of Learning

PSED Personal, social and emotional development
CLL Communication, language and literacy
MD Mathematical development
KUW Knowledge and understanding of the world
PD Physical development
CD Creative development

Myself

Tommy Thumb

To-mmy Thumb, To-mmy Thumb | Where are you? | Here I am, here I am | How do you do?

Pe-ter Poin-ter, Pe-ter Poin-ter | Where are you? | Here I am, here I am | How do you do?

Mi-ddle Man, Mi-ddle Man | Where are you? | Here I am, here I am | How do you do?

Ru-by Ring, Ru-by Ring | Where are you? | Here I am, here I am | How do you do?

Ba-by Small, Ba-by Small | Where are you? | Here I am, here I am | How do you do?

FUN SONGS for the early years: Action songs

Tommy Thumb

Tommy Thumb, Tommy Thumb
(Children hold up both thumbs.)

Where are you?
Here I am, here I am
(Children bend thumbs up and down.)

How do you do?

Peter Pointer, Peter Pointer
(Children hold up both index fingers.)

Where are you?
Here I am, here I am
Children bend index fingers up and down.

How do you do?

Middle Man, Middle Man
(Children hold up both middle fingers.)

Where are you?
Here I am, here I am
(Children bend middle fingers up and down.)

How do you do?

Ruby Ring, Ruby Ring
(Children hold up both third fingers.)

Where are you?
Here I am, here I am
(Children bend third fingers up and down.)

How do you do?

Baby Small, Baby Small
(Children hold up both little fingers.)

Where are you?
Here I am, here I am
(Children bend little fingers up and down.)

How do you do?

Fingers all, fingers all
(Children hold up all fingers.)

Where are you?
Here we are, here we are
(Children open and close all fingers.)

How do you do?

Tommy Thumb
How to use this song

Sharing the song

This song covers the concepts of relating to others, conservation of number, body awareness, and awareness of occupations. It links in with themes such as 'Our friends', 'Let's count', 'Our bodies', and 'People who help us'. Good times to sing it are at your welcome time at the beginning of a session, at the beginning of circle time or after telling a version of the story of *Tom Thumb* from the *Favourite Tales* series (Ladybird Books).

Introduce the song by talking about how people feel happy when someone says 'hello' to them, and that you can also say 'How do you do?'. Make a 'finger family' puppet by stuffing a rubber glove with tissue and drawing a face in felt-tipped pen on each fingertip. Hold up each finger on one of your hands, one at a time, and ask individual children to say 'How do you do, Tommy?' and so on, or 'Hello, Tommy'. Introduce the names of the different fingers used in the song.

Activity ideas

● Point to one finger on the 'finger family' puppet and ask individual children to sing:
   Hello, Tommy, (and so on)
   Hello, Tommy
   How are you?

Sing yourself, in reply:
   Very well, thank you
   Very well, thank you.
   How are you?

Ask the child to reply: 'Fine, thank you, Tommy' (and so on). As a variation, ask one child to sing to another, using their own name. **(CLL)**

● Play conservation games with the 'finger family' puppet, gloves, or the children's fingers. Count the children's fingers both 'squashed together' and 'spread out', showing that the number of fingers is still the same. Use the photocopiable sheet and ask the children to count the fingers and then write the correct numbers in the boxes provided. **(MD)**

● Make a collection of 'finger' items such as rings, thimbles, and finger stalls. **(KUW)**

● Set up a role-play manicurist's shop. Beforehand, let children draw matching designs on five pairs of small, white peel-off labels ('false fingernails'). For the role-play, provide baby lotion for the manicurist to rub onto customers' hands, and a fine paintbrush dipped in a small shampoo bottle filled with water ('colourless nail varnish') to paint their nails. **(CD)**

Tommy Thumb

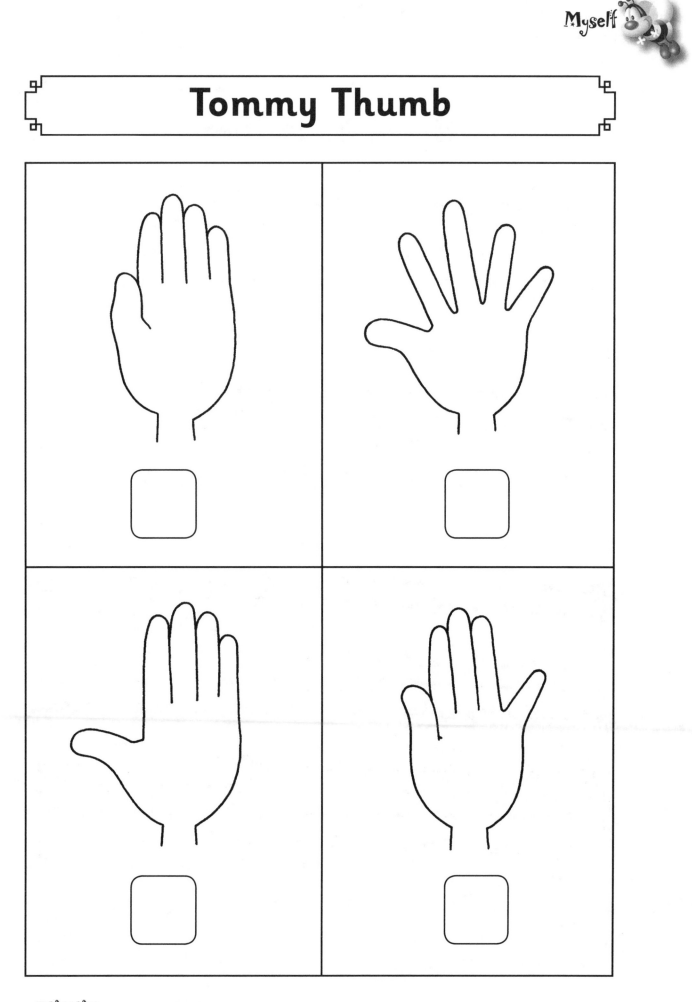

Open, Shut Them

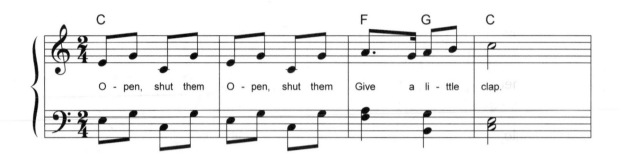

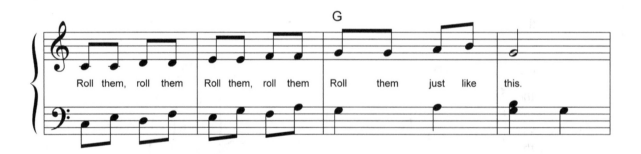

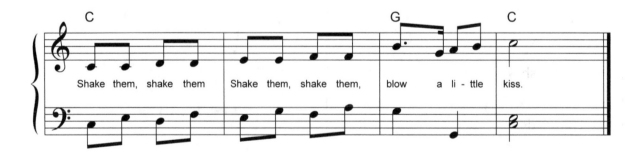

Open, Shut Them

Open, shut them
(Hold hands spread wide, then close in fist.)

Open, shut them
(Hold hands spread wide, then close in fist.)

Give a little clap.
(Clap gently.)

Open, shut them
(Hold hands spread wide, then close in fist.)

Open, shut them
(Hold hands spread wide, then close in fist.)

Lay them in your lap.
(Lay hands down.)

Roll them, roll them
(Roll hands together.)

Roll them, roll them
(Roll hands together.)

Roll them just like this.
(Roll hands together.)

Shake them, shake them
(Shake hands from side to side.)

Shake them, shake them
Shake hands from side to side.)

Blow a little kiss.
(Blow a kiss.)

Open, shut them
(Hold hands spread wide, then close in fist.)

Open, shut them
(Hold hands spread wide, then close in fist.)

Give a little clap.
(Clap gently.)

Open, shut them
(Hold hands spread wide, then close in fist.)

Open, shut them
(Hold hands spread wide, then close in fist.)

Lay them in your lap.
(Lay hands down.)

Roll them, roll them
(Roll hands together.)

Roll them, roll them
(Roll hands together.)

Roll them just like this.
(Roll hands together.)

Shake them, shake them
(Shake hands from side to side.)

Shake them, shake them
(Shake hands from side to side.)

Blow a little kiss.
(Blow a kiss.)

Open, Shut Them
How to use this song

Learning objectives

Stepping Stone
Show curiosity, observe and manipulate objects.

Early Learning Goal
Investigate objects and materials by using all of their senses as appropriate. **(KUW)**

Group size
Eight children.

Props
For each child:
Sock
Child's jumper
Child's coat

Sharing the song

Use the song to develop an understanding of the concept of communicating using hand movements, gesture and writing, as part of themes such as 'Our bodies', 'Our friends', and 'Let's write'.

Sing the song (first three verses) just before a group of children uses playdough and at home time. Introduce the song by talking about how important our hands and fingers are, for example, for holding things, and talk about how they work. Talk about and demonstrate when we open and shut our hands (when dropping and picking up a sock), make a rolling movement (roll up an item of clothing, instead of folding it, when packing) and make a shaking movement (when shaking out a wet coat).

After singing along to the CD, sing the song again, asking all the children to drop and pick up a sock, roll up a jumper, and shake out their coats, when the actions tell them to.

Activity ideas

● Talk about how we can use our hands and fingers to 'talk' to people without saying anything. Invite the children to open and close their fingers to make a 'bye-bye' gesture, and to straighten and bend their index finger to indicate 'please come here'. Think of other examples, such as tapping the forehead to mean 'I'm thinking!'. **(CLL)**

● Talk about 'laps' and 'lap-tops'. Show a real or replica lap-top computer, if possible, and explain how they can be used to send email messages. Encourage the children to talk about why and to whom family members send emails. Ask children to say to whom they would like to send an email, and what they would write. Sing the words below, to the song tune:
　　Open up your lap-top now
　　Keep it on your lap!
　　Send an email straightaway,
　　Tap, tap, tap, tap, tap! **(CLL)**

● Talk about how, when we open and close our hands or fingers, we can call it 'squeezing'. Invite the children to squeeze playdough balls, sponge balls, wet sponges and face cloths, 'bulldog' paper clips, tweezers and 'squeezy' hair clips. Hand out copies of the photocopiable sheet and ask the children to match up the pictures with the relevant piece of equipment. **(KUW)**

Open, Shut Them

One Finger, One Thumb

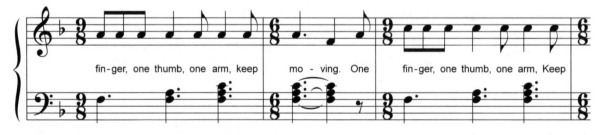

One Finger, One Thumb

One finger, one thumb,
Keep moving.
One finger, one thumb,
Keep moving.
One finger, one thumb,
Keep moving
And we'll all be happy again.

(Hold up one finger, one thumb and move them up and down.)

One finger, one thumb, one arm,
Keep moving.
One finger, one thumb, one arm,
Keep moving.
One finger, one thumb, one arm
Keep moving
And we'll all be happy again.

(Hold up one finger, one thumb and one arm and move them up and down.)

One finger, one thumb, one arm, one leg,
Keep moving.
One finger, one thumb, one arm, one leg,
Keep moving.
One finger, one thumb, one arm, one leg,
Keep moving
And we'll all be happy again.

(Hold up one finger, one thumb, one arm and stand on one leg moving them up and down.)

One finger, one thumb, one arm, one leg,
one nod of the head
Keep moving.
One finger, one thumb, one arm, one leg,
one nod of the head
Keep moving.
One finger, one thumb, one arm, one leg,
one nod of the head
Keep moving.
And we'll all be happy again.

(Hold up one finger, one thumb, one arm and stand on one leg moving them up and down and nodding head.)

Repeat all.

One Finger, One Thumb
How to use this song

card person made with split pins, to show the
different movements. Let the children copy
the movements you make with the model.

Learning objectives

Stepping Stone
Show some understanding that good
practices with regard to exercise, eating,
sleeping and hygiene can contribute to
good health.

Early Learning Goal
Recognise the importance of keeping
healthy and those things which
contribute to this. **(PD)**

Group size
Any size.

Props
Small, jointed, wooden artist's model, or
card person made with split pins.

Sharing the song

The song covers the concepts of exercise,
joints and hinges, body language and using
the body to make prints. Appropriate themes
would be 'Ourselves', 'Keeping fit', 'Feelings',
and 'Pattern'. The song can be used when the
children move from one area to another,
especially when they are going outside or
coming in. (Use the CD player in battery
mode if you are outdoors).

Introduce the song by singing 'Tommy
Thumb' first and then explain that 'One finger,
one thumb' is about Peter Pointer and Tommy
Thumb, and three other parts of our body –
our arm, leg and head. Tell the children that
we are happy when our bodies are healthy,
and that to be healthy, we have to move our
bodies by exercising. Talk about joints in our
fingers, thumbs, elbows, wrists, necks and
knees, which make our bodies bend. Bend a
small, jointed, wooden artist's model
(available from artists' supplies shops), or a
card person made with split pins, to show the
different movements. Let the children copy
the movements you make with the model.

Activity ideas

● Explain that, sometimes, people use their
thumbs, fingers, heads and bodies to show
other people how they are feeling, or to send
a message to them without speaking. Talk
about 'thumbs up' and 'thumbs down', using
Peter Pointer to point
out a direction to
someone who is lost,
waving to say 'bye-bye',
and nodding and
shaking our heads. Talk
about how deaf
people use signing
and how traffic police
use hand signals.
Encourage individual
children to 'sign' or
gesture, for
everyone to guess what they are saying. Next,
hand out copies of the photocopiable sheet
and ask the children to complete the pictures
by adding fingers and thumbs as required.
(CLL)

● Hold up a door hinge and explain that our
joints are like door hinges, and make our
'limbs' move. Go on a 'hinge hunt' around
your setting. **(KUW)**

● Look at pictures of sportspeople and point
out where their joints bend. Let children make
sportspeople from pipe cleaners, bending
them into position. **(KUW)**

● Encourage everyone to cover their
fingertips, thumbs or elbows in a (light)
coloured paint and to make pattern prints on
paper by dabbing or rotating in different
directions. **(CD)**

One Finger, One Thumb

At home

Polly, Put the Kettle On

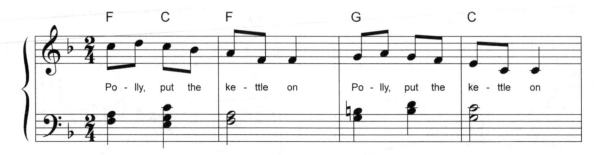

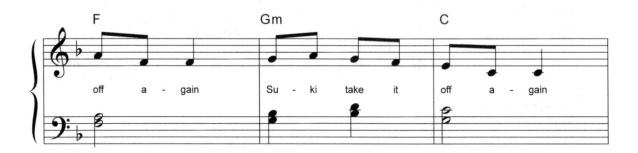

Polly, Put the Kettle On

Polly, put the kettle on
Polly, put the kettle on
Polly, put the kettle on
(Children pretend to hold and move a kettle)

We'll all have tea.
(Pretend to drink tea from a cup.)

Suki take it off again
Suki take it off again
Suki take it off again
(Children pretend to move kettle away)

They've all gone away.
(Wave goodbye.)

Polly, put the kettle on
Polly, put the kettle on
Polly, put the kettle on
(Children pretend to hold and move a kettle)

We'll all have tea.
(Pretend to drink tea from a cup.)

Suki take it off again
Suki take it off again
Suki take it off again
(Children pretend to move kettle away.)

They've all gone away.
(Wave goodbye.)

Polly, put the kettle on
Polly, put the kettle on
Polly, put the kettle on
(Children pretend to hold and move a kettle.)

We'll all have tea.
(Pretend to drink tea from a cup.)

Suki take it off again
Suki take it off again
Suki take it off again
(Children pretend to move kettle away.)

They've all gone away.
(Wave goodbye.)

Polly, Put the Kettle On
How to use this song

Learning objectives

Stepping Stone
Order two items by weight or capacity.

Early Learning Goal
Use language such as 'greater', 'smaller', 'heavier' or 'lighter' to compare quantities. **(MD)**

Group size
Eight children.

Props and costumes
Dolls' kettle
Teacups
Counters

Sharing the song

Use the song to develop the children's understanding of the concepts of capacity ('full' and 'half-full'), one-to-one matching, pouring, infusion and combining media. These concepts can be covered in themes such as 'Food and drink', 'Cafés', 'Let's pretend', 'Celebrations', and 'Touch and texture'.

Provide a dolls' kettle, teapots and teacups in the water tray and play the song on the CD player quietly in the background (at a safe distance) as the children pour.

Introduce the song by playing the CD a few times. Stand the children in a circle on an uncarpeted area (or outside). Ask one child to be Polly and to stand in the centre, holding a dolls' kettle full of water. Ask everyone else to hold a doll's cup with a 'round teabag' (a counter) inside. At the word 'tea', Polly chooses a child, who says 'half (or a full) cup, please'. Polly then pours out accordingly. Choose a second child to be Suki, who will then take the kettle 'off' by taking the kettle from Polly and putting it back on the tray.

Activity ideas

● Explain that when we make tea, we can either pour boiling water from the kettle onto a teabag inside a mug or cup, or we can pour the water into a teapot with teabags inside. (Talk about why children must never touch real kettles or teapots.) Demonstrate, using boiled water, a real kettle, mugs, teapot and square and round teabags, with the children at a safe distance. Talk about using 'one teabag for each person', and say 'How many people would like a cup of tea? How many teabags do we need?'. **(MD)**

● Point out that when we fill a teapot with water from the kettle, the water is colourless, but that when we pour the tea out, the water is a golden colour. Ask if the children know why this happens, and demonstrate by pouring boiling water onto a teabag inside a heatproof glass bowl. **(KUW)**

● Make a display of different spouts, including a kettle, a teapot, milk jug, gravy boat, watering can with long thin spout, and an empty petrol can with retractable spout. Alternatively, leave these in the water tray for the children to explore themselves. Ask the children to cut out the spouts on the photocopiable sheet and to match them with the correct pots. **(KUW)**

● Ask children to spread glue onto paper and then to pour dry sand from a dolls' kettle or teapot slowly onto the paper, to create patterns. **(CD)**

Polly, Put the Kettle On

Pat-a-cake, Pat-a-cake

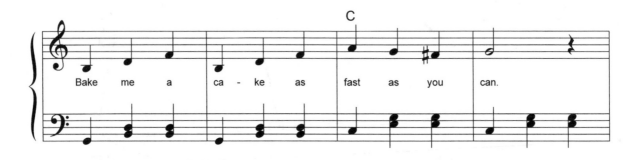

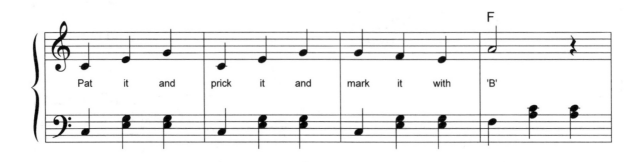

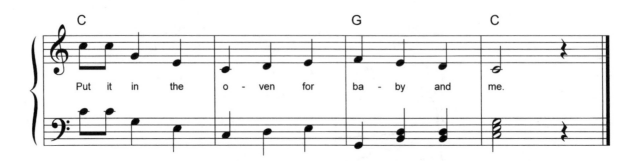

Pat-a-cake, Pat-a-cake

Pat-a-cake, pat-a-cake
Baker's man.
(Pat hands back and forth as though transferring cake from one to the other.)

Bake me a cake as fast as you can.
Pat it and prick it and mark it with 'B'
(Use pencil to score B in play dough cakes.)

Put it in the oven for baby and me.
(Hands placing cake in an oven.)

Pat-a-cake, pat-a-cake
Baker's man.
(Pat hands back and forth as though transferring cake from one to the other.)

Bake me a cake as fast as you can.
Pat it and prick it and mark it with 'B'
(Use pencil to score B in play dough cakes.)

Put it in the oven for baby and me.
(Hands placing cake in an oven.)

Pat-a-cake, pat-a-cake
Baker's man.
(Pat hands back and forth as though transferring cake from one to the other.)

Bake me a cake as fast as you can.
Pat it and prick it and mark it with 'B'
(Use pencil to score B in play dough cakes.)

Put it in the oven for baby and me.
(Hands placing cake in an oven.)

Pat-a-cake, pat-a-cake
Baker's man.
(Pat hands back and forth as though transferring cake from one to the other.)

Bake me a cake as fast as you can.
Pat it and prick it and mark it with 'B'
(Use pencil to score B in play dough cakes.)

Put it in the oven for baby and me.
(Hands placing cake in an oven.)

Pat-a-cake, Pat-a-cake
How to use this song

Learning objectives

Stepping Stone
Begin to form recognisable letters.

Early Learning Goal
Use a pencil and hold it effectively to form recognisable letters, most of which are correctly formed. **(CLL)**

Group size
Six children.

Props
Playdough cakes
Pencils

Sharing the song

Use this song to develop some of the concepts of letter formation, giving comfort to others, subtraction and selling goods. These concepts may be linked to themes such as 'Let's write', 'Caring and sharing', 'Baby clinic', 'Shops', and 'Let's pretend'. You can sing the song as the children make playdough cakes, or use it as part of a cooking activity where children are making real cakes.

Introduce the song by giving each child a playdough 'cake' to pass from the left hand to the right hand, and back again, in a 'pat-a-cake' motion, as they sing along to the CD. Before giving everyone their cake, lightly score a letter 'B' on each one with a pencil. Give the children a pencil so they can each 'mark' their 'cake' at the appropriate lines in the song.

Activity ideas

● Using dolls and soft toy dogs, let children demonstrate how pats can make babies and pets feel happy. **(PSED)**

● Sing the adapted version of the song below, and sing about cakes with a chosen alphabet letter, for different 'scenarios'. For example, the children can be 'zoo keepers', asking the 'zoo baker' to make cakes for the animals and themselves.
(Last two lines of each verse)
   Please write a   --------* very carefully.
   Then we'll eat the cake for our tea!
*say name of a capital letter, or sound of a lower case letter.
Invite the children to cut out the buns on the photocopiable sheet, write in the appropriate letters and then place them in the mouths of the relevant zoo animals. **(CLL)**

● Ask each child to make five playdough cakes and to choose one letter (capital or lower case) to write on all of them. Recite the following words with each child:
   Five pat-a-cakes in a baker's shop
   Round and fat with a -------* on the top
   Along came a boy/girl with a penny one day
   Bought a cake and ate it straightaway.
* Say name of a capital letter or the sound of a lower-case letter.
Ask how many 'pat-a-cakes' are left. **(MD)**

● Cut out a card cake for each child, with their initials written on. Let everyone take turns to be the shopkeeper and sell them to the correct children. **(CD)**

Pat-a-cake, Pat-a-cake

Teddy Bear, Teddy Bear

Te - ddy Bear, Te - ddy Bear Turn a - rou - nd.

Te - ddy Bear, Te - ddy Bear Touch the grou - nd.

Te - ddy Bear, Te - ddy Bear Show your sh - oe.

Te - ddy Bear, Te - ddy Bear That will do.

Teddy Bear, Teddy Bear

Teddy bear, teddy bear
Turn around.
(Arms out to the side and turn around.)

Teddy bear, teddy bear
Touch the ground.
(Bend down to touch the ground.)

Teddy bear, teddy bear
Show your shoe.
(Extend ankle and twist foot to show it off.)

Teddy bear, teddy bear
That will do.
(Put index finger up and wag it.)

Teddy bear, teddy bear
Climb the stairs.
(Pretend to climb upwards.)

Teddy bear, teddy bear
Say your prayers.
(Hands together to pray.)

Teddy bear, teddy bear
Turn out the lights.
(Use index finger to 'switch' off light.)

Teddy bear, teddy bear
Say 'Goodnight'.
(Lay head on hands and close eyes.)

Teddy Bear, Teddy Bear
How to use this song

Learning objectives

Stepping Stone
Show care and concern for self.

Early Learning Goal
Have a developing awareness of their own needs, views and feelings and be sensitive to the needs, views and feelings of others. **(PSED)**

Group size
Eight children.

Props
Teddy bears with 'shoes' (coloured paper strips attached with sticky tape – see illustration)

Sharing the song

The story can be used to develop concepts of self-awareness, behaviour, rhyme, length and circularity in themes such as 'Feelings', 'Helping at home', 'Rhyming fun', 'Shoe shops', and 'Round and round'. Appropriate times for singing are tidy-up time, or after telling a teddy bear story, such as *Where's my Teddy?* by Jez Alborough (Walker Books). Introduce the song by letting each of the children hold a teddy bear. They can then teach it to do the actions. Ask everyone to talk about how bears (or other soft toys) make them feel happy, especially at bedtime. Talk about bedtime routines, especially tidying up bedrooms, and how family members can feel if we do not help. When singing the song independently, add the following lines, after 'prayers':
Teddy bear, teddy bear, put your toys away
Tidy and ready for another day.
Using the photocopiable sheet, invite the children to cut out the teddy bear and toys

and to stick a lollipop stick to the teddy. Add a piece of Blu-tack on the back of the three toys and place them on teddy's bedroom floor. Stick Blu-tack on teddy's paw and show the children how to help teddy tidy up by picking up the toys and sticking them in the toy box provided. Ask everyone to 'teach' the bears what to do at tidy-up time.

Activity ideas

● Provide three pairs of rhyming objects (such as a doll's coat/ toy boat; a hat/ doormat; a spoon/ balloon) and ask the children to make up new words to the song, such as:
Teddy bear, teddy bear, put on your coat
Teddy bear, teddy bear, sit in the boat.
(CLL)

● Stuff three pairs of socks (baby, toddler and child-sized) with tissue. Ask the children to stick them on teddy bears of appropriate sizes with sticky tape, and to find shoes of the right size. **(MD)**

● Make 'twirling bears' using card bears attached with string to straws. Ask the children to twist the string to make the bears twirl and dance around. Investigate other kinds of spinners, such as gyroscopes, spinning tops and sycamore keys. **(KUW).**

● Talk about the importance of turning out the lights at night time, in order not to waste electricity. Go on a 'light switch hunt' around your setting. Ask children to write labels saying 'Please remember to switch off!'. Talk about never playing with switches and sockets. **(KUW)**

Teddy Bear, Teddy Bear

Let's move!

The Grand Old Duke of York

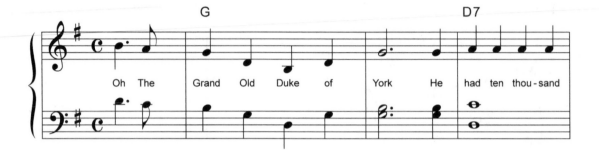

Oh The | Grand Old Duke of | York He | had ten thou-sand

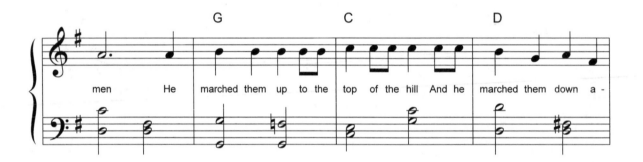

men He | marched them up to the | top of the hill And he | marched them down a-

gain. And | when they were up they were | up. And | when they were down They were

down And | when they were on-ly | half-way up They were | nei-ther up nor | down.

The Grand Old Duke of York

The Grand Old Duke of York
He had ten thousand men.
He marched them up to the top of the hill
(March with arms by side 'up' the chalked hill.)

And he marched them down again.
(March with arms by side 'down' the chalked hill.)

And when they were up
They were up.
(March with arms by side 'up' the chalked hill.)

And when they were down
They were down
(March with arms by side 'down' the chalked hill.)

And when they were only half-way up
They were neither up nor down.
(Stand still halfway down the chalked hill.)

(Repeat four times)

The Grand Old Duke of York
How to use this song

Learning objectives

Stepping Stone
Move in a range of ways, such as slithering, shuffling, rolling, crawling, walking, running, jumping, skipping, sliding and hopping.

Early Learning Goal
Move with confidence, imagination and in safety. **(PD)**

Group size
Eight children.

Props
Chalk or tailor's chalk
Hat with feathers

Sharing the song

This song introduces the ideas of movement, responding to instructions, decision-making and spatial awareness. These concepts can be explored in themes such as 'Let's move', 'Our bodies', 'Jobs', and 'Journeys'. Use the song when the children are moving from one area to another, both indoors and outdoors.

To introduce the song draw a sloping line (a hill) with chalk, if outside, or with tailor's chalk on carpet, if inside. Practise marching on the spot, with everyone swinging their arms. Play the CD, with soldiers individually, or one behind the other, in pairs or groups of three or four, depending on space, marching up, down and halfway along the line. When doing this activity without the CD, you or a child can wear the hat and be the Duke, giving orders to march quickly or slowly, or to jump, hop, skip, jog, stride or walk on tip-toes. The soldiers can also move in a variety of ways, in response to different percussion instruments.

Activity ideas

● Play 'Listening soldiers' asking the children to respond to army orders, given by another child (the Duke), such as 'Quick march!', 'Left, right, left, right!', 'About turn', 'Salute!', 'Attention!', 'Stand at ease!' and 'Stand easy!' (see illustration). **(CLL)**

● Encourage each child to tell a very simple story involving changing their mind, such as 'One morning, I decided to have cornflakes for breakfast. Then I changed my mind, so I had a boiled egg with toast soldiers instead'. **(CLL)**

● Teach 'left' and 'right' by letting children wear lemon (left) and red (right) coloured paper bracelets and anklets, on which are written 'left' and 'right'. Play directional games involving turning left and right, using arrows chalked in lemon and red. **(MD)**

● Using a length of 'roadway', two small-world play people and two toy mobile phones, encourage a pair of children to have a conversation about the play people meeting each other halfway along the road. Alternatively, use a roadway playmat, and ask the children to identify specific buildings which are halfway along a particular 'street', so that the play people may 'meet' in front of the building. **(MD)**

● Make copies of the photocopiable sheet, one for each child, and cut out the soldier outline and the holes. Invite the children to colour in their soldier shapes and show them how to push their fingers through the holes to make their soldier 'march'. Ask them to pretend their Peter Pointer is the soldier's left foot and their Finger Tall is the soldier's right foot. Let them march their soldiers around the track, saying 'left, right' and turning the paper as they go. **(PD)**

The Grand Old Duke of York

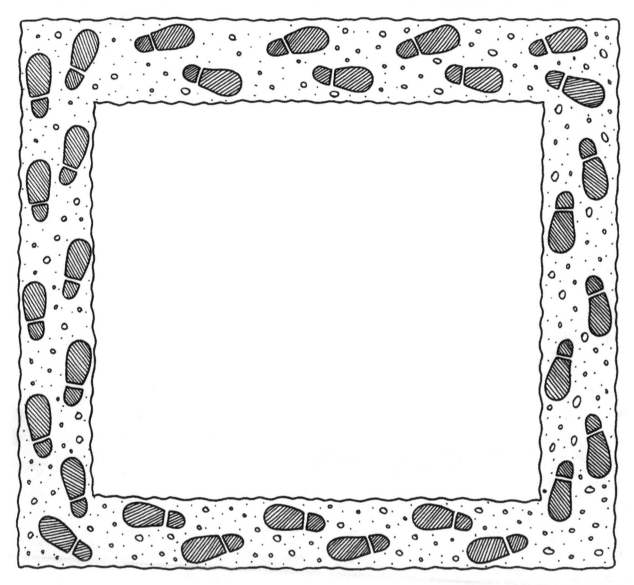

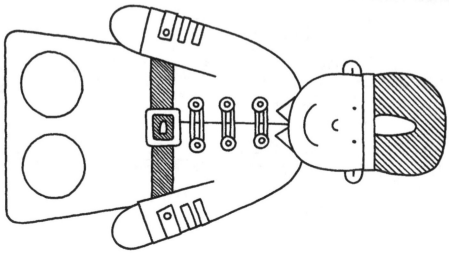

Row, Row, Row Your Boat

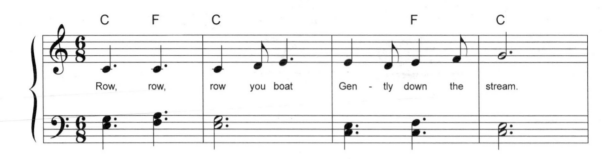

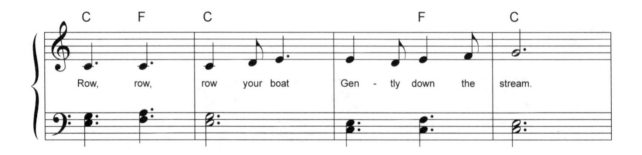

Row, Row, Row Your Boat

(Children sit in pairs on the floor, facing each other, legs extended and holding hands.)

Row, row, row your boat
Gently down the stream.
(Gently pull back and forth, leaning in and out.)

Merrily, merrily, merrily, merrily
Life is but a dream.

Row, row, row your boat
Gently down the stream.
(Gently pull back and forth, leaning in and out.)

If you see a crocodile
Don't forget to scream!
(Hold hands to mouth and let out a gentle scream.)

Row, Row, Row Your Boat
How to use this song

Learning objectives

Stepping Stone
Operate equipment by means of pushing and pulling movements.

Early Learning Goal
Use a range of small and large equipment. **(PD)**

Group size
Eight children.

Props
'Oars' made from aluminium foil tubes and card.

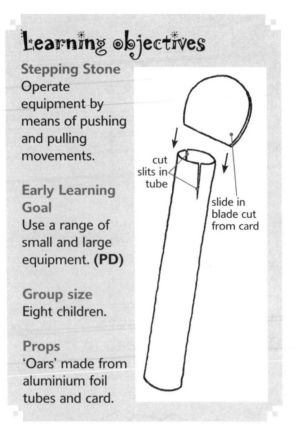

cut slits in tube

slide in blade cut from card

Sharing the song

Use this song to explore the concepts of different 'push' and 'pull' forces, dreaming, water transport and transporting loads. Develop these concepts in themes such as 'Water', 'Transport', 'Imagination', 'Day and night' and 'Wheels'.

Children can enjoy singing the song during water play, when, for example, they are using boats containing play people holding 'oars' (short pieces of straws attached with sticky tape). Additionally, in an outside sandpit, pairs of children can mould a 'rowing boat' large enough for two children to sit opposite each other, while singing the song.

When introducing the song, ask children to sit facing each other in pairs, holding hands. Ask everyone to move backwards and forwards as they sing. At other times, ask the children to drop hands, and give one child (the rower) a pair of oars. Ask them to 'row' the other child, and then to change places.

Activity ideas

● Talk about dreams we have at night, and daydreams, when we pretend happy things are happening in our imaginations. Say that people can have daydreams when they are being rowed gently, in a rowing boat, down a stream. Ask everyone to close their eyes and pretend they are gliding along in a boat, down a stream, having a lovely daydream. Ask everyone to talk about their daydream. **(CLL)**

● Find pictures of different kinds of rowing boats, such as one-person skiffs, two-seater rowing boats, galleys, canoes and kayaks. Let the children use recycled materials to make models, for example, plastic date boxes or margarine tubs for boats, and glue spreaders, straws, lollipop sticks or coffee stirrers for oars. **(KUW)**

● Ask the children to sort the outside wheeled toys into those requiring pushing and those requiring pulling. **(KUW)**

● Invite the children to cut out pictures from magazines and catalogues of items which are pushed or pulled, to stick inside a large book (push – baby buggy, pram, tea trolley, supermarket trolley, wheelbarrow, wheelybin; pull – suitcase on wheels, shopping-bag trolley, post person's trolley, pull-along toy). **(KUW)**

● Hand out copies of the photocopiable sheet and look at the pictures together. Read the two words 'push' and 'pull' and talk about what they mean, demonstrating the actions. Now ask the children to draw a line from each picture to one of the words to say how it is moved. **(KUW)**

Row, Row, Row Your Boat

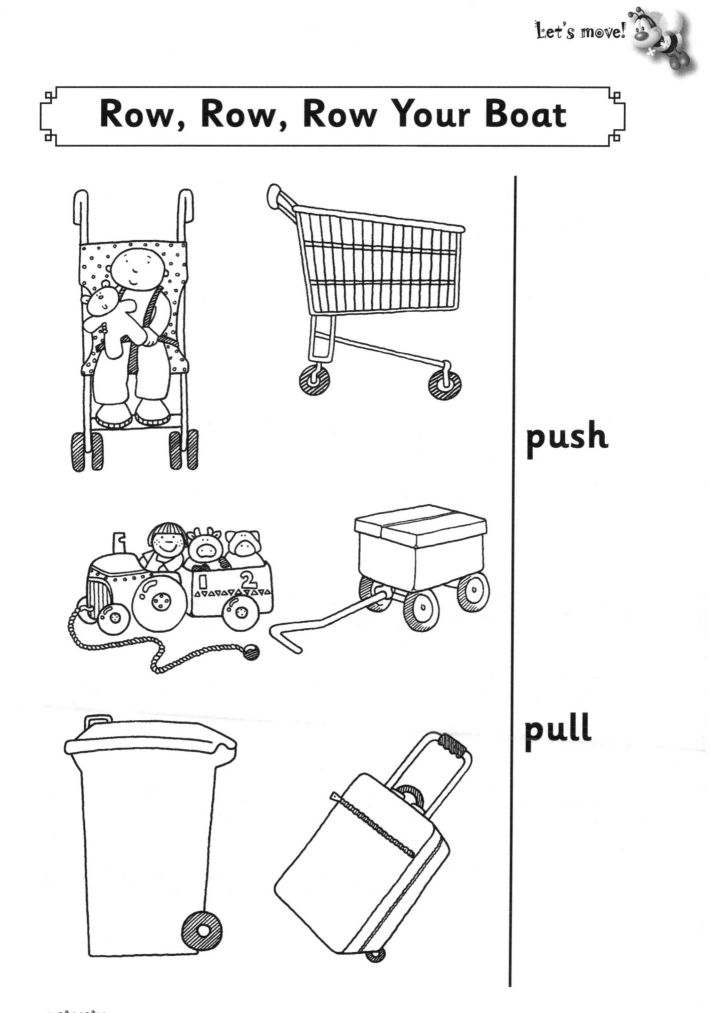

push

pull

Wind Your Bobbin Up

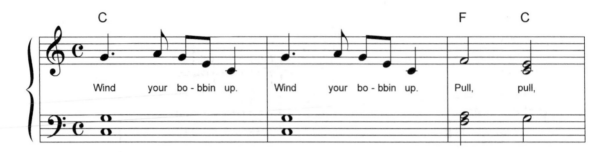

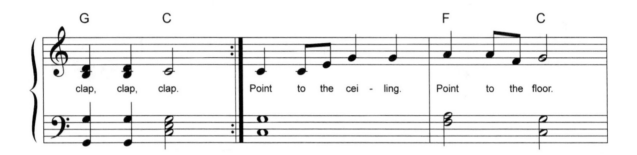

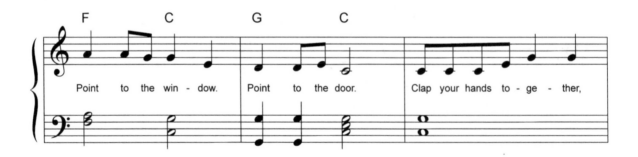

Wind Your Bobbin Up

Wind your bobbin up.
Wind your bobbin up.
(Extend arms forward and roll one over the other.)

Pull, pull, clap, clap, clap.
(Pulling movement with both hands and then clap.)

Wind your bobbin up.
Wind your bobbin up.
(Extend arms forward and roll one over the other.)

Pull, pull, clap, clap, clap.
(Pulling movement with both hands and then clap.)

(Point to the parts of the room in turn.)

Point to the ceiling.
Point to the floor.
Point to the window.
Point to the door.
Clap your hands together, one, two, three.
(Clap hands.)

Put your hands upon your knee.
(Place hands on knees.)

Wind it back again.
Wind it back again.
(Extend arms forward and roll back the other way.)

Pull, pull, clap, clap, clap.
(Pulling movement with both hands and then clap.)

Wind it back again.
Wind it back again.
(Extend arms forward and roll back the other way.)

Pull, pull, clap, clap, clap.
(Pulling movement with both hands and then clap.)

(Point to the parts of the room in turn.)

Point to the ceiling.
Point to the floor.
Point to the window.
Point to the door.
Clap your hands together, one, two, three.
(Clap hands.)

Put your hands upon your knee.
(Place hands on knees.)

(Repeat)

Wind Your Bobbin Up
How to use this song

Sharing the song

Use this song to develop the concepts of direction, fabric manufacture, spirals, and awareness of occupations in themes such as 'Forwards and backwards', 'Clothes', 'Pattern and shape', and 'Jobs'.

The song is useful to sing when a group of children is finishing using threading beads or sewing shapes. Ask the children to unthread their necklaces or shapes, and to wind the laces around small pieces of card in order to keep the laces untangled. Ask pairs of children to sit opposite each other. Give one child a plastic threading cotton reel (the bobbin) with the end of a lace wrapped around it, secured with sticky tape. Ask the other child to hold the end of the fully extended lace. The whole group sing as they wind up and wind back the bobbin, before changing places.

Activity ideas

● At tidy-up time, let everyone sing the version below, as they tidy:
   Let's all tidy up (repeat twice)
   Carefully!
   Let's all tidy up (repeat twice)
   Quickly!
(PSED)
● Hold up a videocassette with the tape

rewound to the beginning. Point out the direction the spools spin in, when the videotape is winding forward, and the direction of the spools when the video is rewinding (winding back). Ask everyone to try to be videotapes, carrying out simple actions as they wind forward and rewind, going backward, such as sitting on a chair, standing up and walking. Individual children could also try to be a video in fast forward mode, and carry out the actions very quickly. **(KUW)**

● Hand out copies of the photocopiable sheet. Show the children how to cut along the dotted lines and then thread the car strip through the slots on the road, like a video filmstrip. Show them how to move the strip to make the car go forwards and then how to rewind by moving it back the other way.
(KUW)

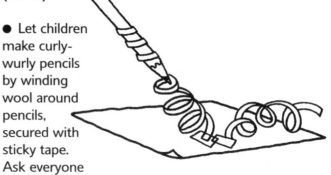

● Let children make curly-wurly pencils by winding wool around pencils, secured with sticky tape. Ask everyone to roll the pencils, so that the wool spirals appear to be moving (see illustration). Children could also make 'curly-wurly' sculptures with silver foil (see illustration).
(KUW)

● When children are winding bandages around patients in hospital play, or winding people's hair around rollers in hairdressing play, change the words of the song to:
   Wind the bandage (hair) up (repeat)
   Pull, pull – but not too tight!
   Wind the bandage (hair) up (repeat)
   Make it snug – that's just right!
(CD)

Wind Your Bobbin Up

Musical fun

Here We Go Round the Mulberry Bush

Here we go round the mul - berry bush, The mul - berry bush, the

mul - berry bush. Here we go round the mul - berry bush, On a

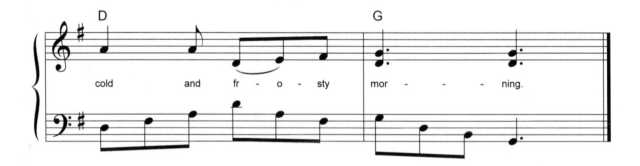

cold and fr - o - sty mor - - - ning.

Here We Go Round the Mulberry Bush

(Children stand in a circle and hold hands.)

Here we go round the mulberry bush,
(Walk around in a circle.)

The mulberry bush, the mulberry bush.
Here we go round the mulberry bush,
On a cold and frosty morning.

(Children stand and clap hands.)

This is the way we clap our hands,
Clap our hands, clap our hands.
This is the way we clap our hands,
On a cold and frosty morning.

(Children stand and stamp feet.)

This is the way we stamp our feet,
Stamp our feet, stamp our feet.
This is the way we stamp our feet,
On a cold and frosty morning.

(Children move around in the circle, skipping.)

This is the way we dance around,
Dance around, dance around.
This is the way we dance around,
On a cold and frosty morning.

(Children stand and stretch up.)

This is the way we stretch up high,
Stretch up high, stretch up high.
This is the way we stretch up high,
On a cold and frosty morning.

(Repeat)

Here We Go Round the Mulberry Bush

How to use this song

Learning objectives

Stepping Stone
Sing to themselves and make up simple songs.

Early Learning Goal
Recognise and explore how sounds can be changed, sing simple songs from memory, recognise repeated sounds and sound patterns and match movements to music. **(CD)**

Group size
Ten children.

Sharing the song

Use this song to help develop the children's understanding of concepts such as frosty weather, body awareness, and also (using the alternative song words below) the change in fruit resulting from baking. The song can also be successfully used in role-play. Appropriate themes are 'Weather', 'Our bodies', 'Clothes', 'Food', 'Farms' and 'People who help us'. The song is useful to sing at the beginning of circle time.

Introduce the song by gathering the children in a circle to sing along to the CD. Enjoy acting out the song together, and then say that the actions they have made are what we do on a cold and frosty morning, to try to warm up. Explain that frost is frozen dew. Ask how we feel and what we look like when we are cold. Say it is fun to change the words of songs, and ask everyone to think of actions we could sing about for a hot and sunny afternoon. Ask everyone to join in the suggested movements.

Activity ideas

● Put a soft toy pet animal in a basket in the centre of the circle. Ask everyone to think of words and actions about looking after the animal. **(PSED)**

● Bring in some silk material for the children to handle. Explain that silkworms make the silk thread, and that they have to eat a lot of leaves from mulberry bushes to be healthy enough to do this. **(KUW)**

● Make an apple tree by hanging apples on string loops from a small, synthetic Christmas tree. Ask everyone to make up words and actions about being apple farmers picking the apples, and then washing, preparing and baking them in apple pies. **(KUW)**

● Put a dressing-up rack or box in the centre of the circle. Ask everyone to move around holding hands and singing 'Here we go round the dressing-up rack/box'. Ask one child at a time to put on an outfit, and everyone else to think of appropriate words and actions about being that person, for example with a doctor's outfit, 'This is the way we take a pulse' and so on. **(CD)**

● Give each child a copy of the photocopiable sheet. Help them to cut out the child and the clothes. Stick the child shape onto a piece of card that is folded over so that it can stand up. Let them colour in the clothes and then show them how to attach this piece using Blu-tack. Let the children hold up their models as you sing the song. Extend by drawing around the clothes outline, cutting out the shape and inviting the children to design new outfits for the model, perhaps to go with their new summer song. **(CD)**

Here We Go Round the Mulberry Bush

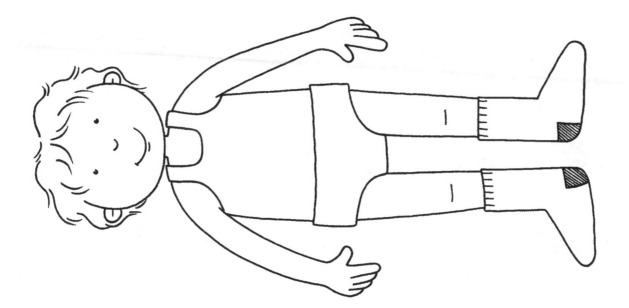

There Was a Princess Long Ago

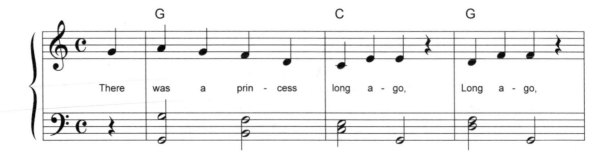

There was a prin-cess long a-go, Long a-go,

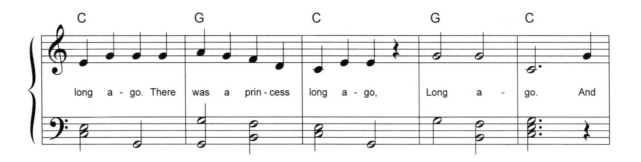

long a-go. There was a prin-cess long a-go, Long a-go. And

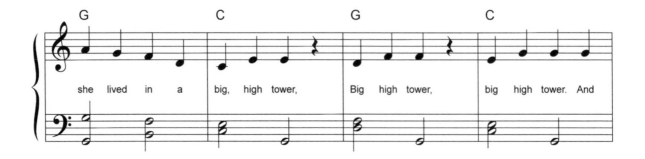

she lived in a big, high tower, Big high tower, big high tower. And

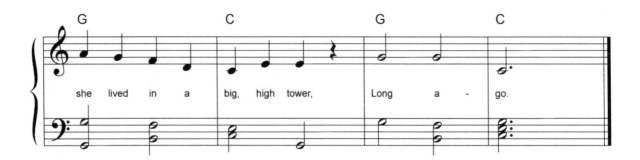

she lived in a big, high tower, Long a-go.

There Was a Princess Long Ago

(Choose a child to be the princess who stands in the middle.
Hold hands above head and link fingers to form a crown.)

There was a princess long ago,
Long ago, long ago.
There was a princess long ago,
Long ago.

(Stretch arms up high.)

And she lived in a big, high tower
Big high tower, big high tower.
And she lived in a big, high tower,
Long ago.

(Stretch one arm, holding a 'wand'.)

One day a fairy waved her wand,
Waved her wand, waved her wand.
One day a fairy waved her wand,
Long ago.

(Close eyes and rest head on hands.)

The princess slept for 100 years,
100 years, 100 years.
The princess slept for 100 years,
Long ago.

(Stretch arms out to side.)

A great, big forest grew around,
Grew around, grew around.
A great, big forest grew around,
Long ago.

(Choose a child to ride around the circle on a hobby horse.
Hold hands up and trot.)

A handsome prince came riding by,
Riding by, riding by.
A handsome prince came riding by
Long ago.

(Stretch both hands out together and make scything movement.)

He took his sword and cut it down,
Cut it down, cut it down.
He took his sword and cut it down,
Long ago.

(Place one hand inside the other.)

He took her hand to wake her up,
Wake her up, wake her up.
He took her hand to wake her up,
Long ago.

(All clap hands.)

So everybody's happy now,
Happy now, happy now.
So everybody's happy now
Long ago.

There Was a Princess Long Ago
How to use this song

Learning objectives

Stepping Stone
Play cooperatively as part of a group to act out a narrative.

Early Learning Goal
Use their imagination in art and design, music, dance, imaginative and role play and stories. **(CD)**

Group size
Ten children.

Props
Crowns and dressing-up clothes Hobby-horse.

Sharing the song

Use this song to develop concepts such as fantasy, consideration, reading one word at a time and the combining of different natural media. Appropriate themes would be 'Let's pretend!', 'Caring and sharing', 'Favourite songs' and 'Holidays'. The song is ideal for singing at story time, after reading a version of *Sleeping Beauty*, perhaps from the *Favourite Tales* series (Ladybird Books). The song can also be used during outdoor play, around a climbing frame disguised as a castle (see illustration). To introduce the song, talk about how, long ago, princes and princesses lived in castles and palaces, and how some still do. Ask everyone to stand in a circle.

Choose a child to dress up and be the princess who stands in the middle, as everyone sings along to the CD and makes the appropriate actions. Continue with the arrival of the prince on a hobby horse.

Activity ideas

● Talk about when and how people should be woken up, for example about being considerate about not disturbing people (babies and parents in the early morning). Talk also about gentle ways to rouse people, without startling them. **(PSED)**

● Write out the words to the song on large sheets of paper attached to an easel. Point to each word with a ruler as the children sing. Ask everyone to sing a word only when the ruler points to the word, one at a time. To demonstrate, ask everyone to sing too quickly, showing that the ruler cannot keep up. **(CLL)**

● Give each child a copy of the photocopiable sheet, cut along the lines and put the pictures in the correct order to tell the story. Staple them in place to make a book. Ask children to use the book to retell the story. **(CLL)**

● Talk about building castles and palaces on the beach at holiday times. Ask everyone for ideas about what to use for recreating Sleeping Beauty's palace and forest in an indoor sand tray, or outside sandpit (for example shells for window, twigs or privet cuttings for the forest). **(CD)**

There Was a Princess Long Ago

I am the Music Man

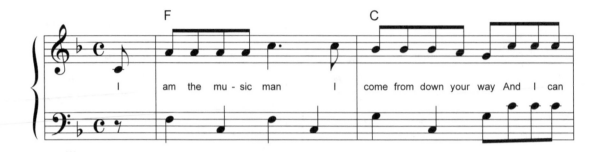

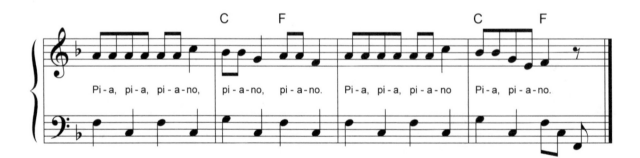

I am the Music Man

I am the music man
I come from down your way
And I can play.
What can you play?

I play the pi-an-o
Pi-a, pi-a, pi-an-o, pi-an-o pi-an-o.
Pi-a, pi-a, pi-an-o, pi-a, pi-an-o.
(Children play an imaginary piano.)

I am the music man
I come from down your way
And I can play.
What can you play?

I play the vi-o-lin
Vi-o, vi-o, vi-o-lin, vi-o-lin, vi-o-lin.
Vi-o, vi-o, vi-o-lin, vi-o, vi-o-lin.
(Children play an imaginary violin.)

Pi-a, pi-a, pi-an-o, pi-an-o pi-an-o.
Pi-a, pi-a, pi-an-o, pi-a, pi-an-o.
(Children play an imaginary piano.)

I am the music man
I come from down your way
And I can play.
What can you play?

I play the saxo-phone
Saxo, saxo, saxo-phone, saxo-phone,
saxo-phone
Saxo, saxo, saxo-phone, saxo, saxo-
phone.
(Children play an imaginary saxophone.)

Vi-o, vi-o, vi-o-lin, vi-o-lin, vi-o-lin.
Vi-o, vi-o, vi-o-lin, vi-o, vi-o-lin.
(Children play an imaginary violin.)

Pi-a, pi-a, pi-an-o, pi-an-o pi-an-o.
Pi-a, pi-a, pi-an-o, pi-a, pi-an-o.
(Children play an imaginary piano.)

I am the music man
I come from down your way
And I can play.
What can you play?

I play the picco-lo
Picco, picco, picco-lo, picco-lo, picco-lo.
Picco, picco, picco-lo, picco, picco-lo.
(Children play an imaginary piccolo.)

Saxo, saxo, saxo-phone, saxo-phone,
saxo-phone.
Saxo, saxo, saxo-phone, saxo, saxo-
phone.
(Children play an imaginary saxophone.)

Vi-o, vi-o, vi-o-lin, vi-o-lin, vi-o-lin.
Vi-o, vi-o, vi-o-lin, vi-o, vi-o-lin.
(Children play an imaginary violin.)

Pi-a, pi-a, pi-an-o, pi-an-o pi-an-o.
Pi-a, pi-a, pi-an-o, pi-a, pi-an-o.
(Children play an imaginary piano.)

I am the Music Man
How to use this song

Learning objectives

Stepping Stone
Show an interest in the way musical instruments sound.

Early Learning Goal
Recognise and explore how sounds can be changed, sing simple songs from memory, recognise repeated sounds and sound patterns and match movements to music. **(CD)**

Group size
Any size.

Sharing the song

This song covers concepts of sound-making, mental counting, adapting song words and physical control and coordination in themes such as 'How does it work?', 'Listening', 'Song fun' and 'Let's move'. Use the song during any musical session, or when you are on the move. Talk about what a portable piano-accordion is and show a picture if possible.

Introduce the song by showing examples of the instruments, if possible, or pictures. Talk about how piano keys are pressed, a violin's strings are scraped, a saxophone is blown from the top and a piccolo is blown from the side. Find percussion instruments which are also tapped or scraped, and look for pictures of instruments blown from the top and side.

Give out copies of the photocopiable sheet and cut out the instruments. Invite the children to stick them under the correct headings. Talk about whether people usually sit or stand to play the various instruments.

Play the CD, asking everyone to sit or stand, according to what they decided, and to sing along and make the appropriate 'playing' movements.

Activity ideas

● Talk about how sometimes we have to count people or things which we cannot touch, and that we do this counting 'in our head'. Say that counting sounds, such as clapping, can help us to learn how to count 'in our head'. Clap different lines from the song, for everyone to count the claps. **(MD)**

● Make up alternative words, such as postperson, newsperson, milkman, ice-cream man. **(CLL)**

I am your post-person
I come from down your way
I can del-iver, del-iver your letters!
Open up the letter-box,
Letter-box, letter-box,
Open up the letter-box
And push the letters through!

● Talk about the careful preliminary actions musicians must make before starting to play, for example, a pianist sitting down and opening the piano lid, or a violinist taking the violin out of the case. Let children take turns to mime a sequence of movements about playing an instrument, for others to guess. **(PD)**

I am the Music Man

Animal fun

Incy Wincy Spider

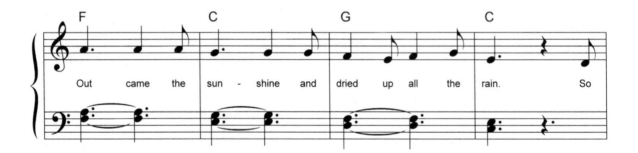

Incy Wincy Spider

Incy Wincy spider
Climbed up the water spout.
(Raise arms above head and join fingertips.)

Down came the raindrops
And washed poor Incy out.
(Bring arms down with pitter-patter finger movements.)

Out came the sunshine
And dried up all the rain.
(Raise arms, join fingers and make circle shape.)

So Incy Wincy spider
Climbed up the spout again.
(Spread fingers and walk one hand against the other upwards.)

Incy Wincy spider
Climbed up the water spout.
(Raise arms above head and join fingertips.)

Down came the raindrops
And washed poor Incy out.
(Bring arms down with pitter-patter finger movements.)

Out came the sunshine
And dried up all the rain.
(Raise arms, join fingers and make circle shape.)

So Incy Wincy spider
Climbed up the spout again.
(Spread fingers and walk one hand against the other upwards.)

Incy Wincy spider
Climbed up the water spout.
(Raise arms above head and join fingertips.)

Down came the raindrops
And washed poor Incy out.
(Bring arms down with pitter-patter finger movements.)

Out came the sunshine
And dried up all the rain.
(Raise arms, join fingers and make circle shape.)

So Incy Wincy spider
Climbed up the spout again.
(Spread fingers and walk one hand against the other upwards.)

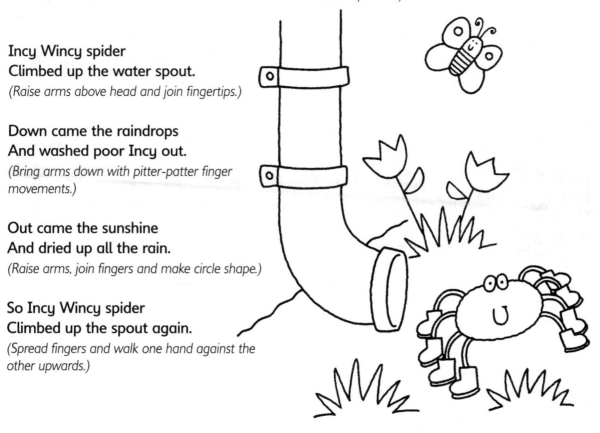

Incy Wincy Spider
How to use this song

Learning objectives

Stepping Stone
Show care and concern for others, for living things and the environment.

Early Learning Goal
Consider the consequences of their words and actions for themselves and others. **(PSED)**

Group size
Any size.

Props
Dolls' jugs
Short pieces of plastic drainpipe or cooking foil tubes
Plastic spiders on string
Doll
Dolls' bath.

Sharing the song

The song can be used to develop concepts of empathy, rain collection, evaporation, and web spinning in themes such as 'Feelings', 'Buildings', 'Weather', and 'Minibeasts'. Sing the song during water play, as children use dolls' jugs to pour 'rain' down plastic drainpipes or cooking foil tubes, with small plastic spiders inside on string. Play the CD quietly in the background, at a safe distance from the water tray.

Sing the song when there are puddles, and when the puddles have all gone. Introduce the song by talking about how, sometimes, a spider will come up a plughole, and how we should not be afraid. Ask what we should say to someone who is afraid of spiders. Sit a doll in a dolls' bath. Ask a child to dangle a plastic spider on a string, and to explain to the doll that there is nothing to be afraid of.

Give each child a copy of the photocopiable sheet and ask them to draw a picture of themselves smiling in the bath. Next, make a hole at the black dots and thread a piece of string through the holes, tying knots on the back to secure it. Cut out the spider and stick it on a piece of Blu-tack, join the spider to the string and pull the string to make the spider move along the bath.

Activity ideas

● Let a child demonstrate how to set a spider free kindly, by placing a plastic tumbler on top of a plastic spider, covering it with a piece of paper, and letting it go. **(PSED)**

● Spot drainpipes and gutters on your building. Ask children to attach drinking straws to dolls' houses with Blu-tack or sticky tape. **(KUW)**

● Attach round, yellow card sun-shapes to the tops of drinking straws with sticky tape. Let children suck up water, 'rain', from saucers, just as the sun sucks up rain from puddles. **(KUW)**

● Talk about how spiders spin webs. Look for webs outside, and in information books. Let children weave webs round the tops of small, upturned chairs, using thick black wool. **(PD)**

Incy, Wincy Spider

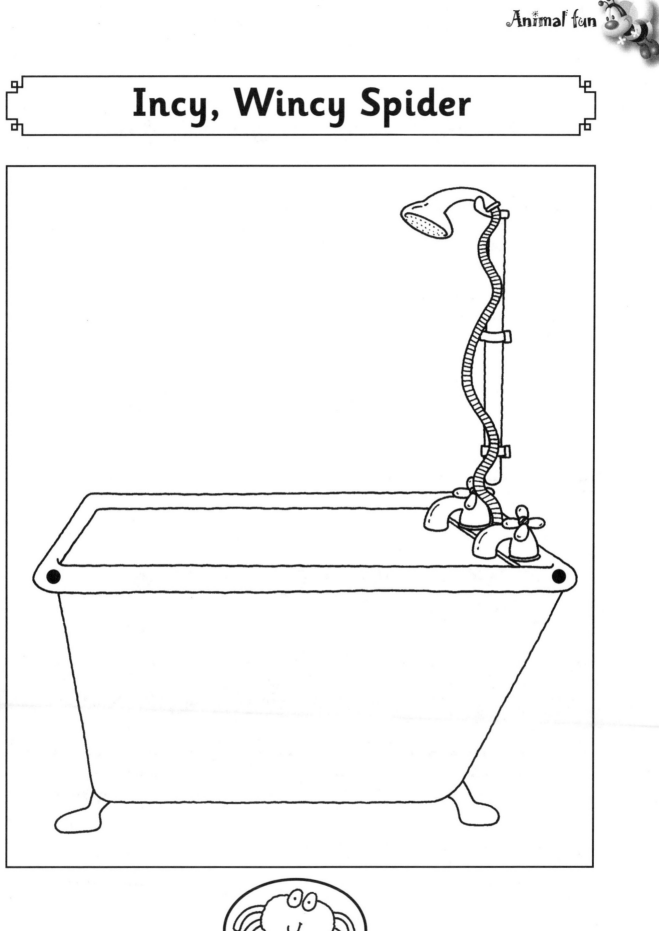

We're Going on a Bear Hunt

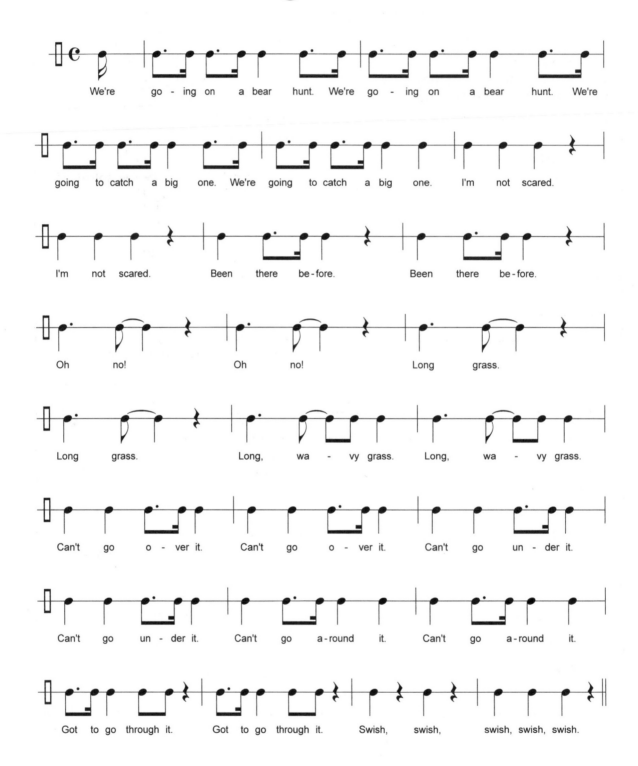

We're Going on a Bear Hunt

We're going on a bear hunt.
We're going on a bear hunt.
We're going to catch a big one.
We're going to catch a big one.
(Raise shoulders and reach arms out to side.)

I'm not scared.
I'm not scared.
Been there before.
Been there before.
Oh no!
Oh no!
Long grass.
Long grass.
Long, wavy grass.
Long, wavy grass.
(Raise arms up and wave from side to side.)

Can't go over it.
Can't go over it.
Can't go under it.
Can't go under it.
Can't go around it.
Can't go around it.
Got to go through it.
Got to go through it.
Swish, swish, swish, swish, swish.

Verse 2
Mud!
Mud!
Thick, squelchy mud.
Thick, squelchy mud.
(Lift leg as if stepping in mud.)

Shlurp, shlurp, shlurp, shlurp, shlurp.
(Shuffle feet.)

Verse 3
A river.
A river.
A deep, swirling river.
A deep swirling river.
(Twirl around.)

Splash, splash, splash, splash, splash.

Verse 4
A cave.
A cave.
A dark, gloomy cave.
A dark, gloomy cave.
(Cup hands over eyes.)

Clunk, clunk, clunk, clunk, clunk.

Verse 5
What's that?
What's that?
Two furry ears.
Two furry ears
Two sharp teeth.
Two sharp teeth
It's a bear.
(Hold up hands to make ears. Bare teeth.)

Quickly, through the cave.
Clunk, clunk, clunk, clunk, clunk.
Through the river.
Splash, splash, splash, splash, splash.
Through the mud.
Shlurp, shlurp, shlurp, shlurp, shlurp
Through the grass.
Swish, swish, swish, swish, swish

Run quickly.
Hold the door.
BANG!

We're Going on a Bear Hunt
How to use this song

Sharing the song

This song is useful for exploring concepts such as position and direction, sounds, and fantasy, in themes such as 'Journeys', 'What can we hear?' and 'Let's pretend'. Sing it during outdoor play, and link with stories about journeys, such as *The Last Bit Bear* by Sandra Chisholm Robinson (Roberts Rinehart), or when children are playing with small-world items or with sand play.

Introduce the song by playing the CD for the children to listen to. Ask them to draw a large-scale bear country outside, using coloured chalk for the long, wavy grass, and so on. Using a CD recorder in battery mode, play the CD again, and ask everyone to go on a bear hunt, one behind the other, pretending to be the bear yourself.

Activity ideas

● Ask each child in turn to verbalise their own journey to your setting, and to include sound effects, for example:

Walk up the path – trip, trap, trip, trap!
Into the car, fasten seat belt – clunk, click!
Off we go! – Brrrumm, brrrumm!
Here we are – unfasten seat belt – clunk, click!

Run down the path – pitter, patter, pitter, patter!
Ring the bell – ding, ding, ding, ding!
Hello!
(CLL)

● Hand out copies of the photocopiable sheet and ask the children to carefully follow the path with a pencil, to show the way to the cave and then back again. **(CLL)**

● Play a game called 'We walk', to develop understanding of the use of prepositions. Draw simple outline drawings on card (one quarter of A4 size) of a gate, a pavement, a road, a tree, a bridge, and a tunnel. Put the cards in a drawstring bag. Ask children, in turn, to pick a card and say, for example, 'We walk along a pavement', or 'We walk across a road', 'under a tree' and so on. **(MD)**

● Ask children to contribute ideas for making sound effects for the rhyme, such as rubbing their palms across paper to create a swishing sound for grass. **(KUW)**

● Create a small-world bear country in a sand tray or sand pit, using, for example, green pipe cleaners for grass, and an old bowl full of mud. Ask everyone to think of exciting things that could happen on the journey. **(CD)**

We're Going on a Bear Hunt

Five Little Monkeys

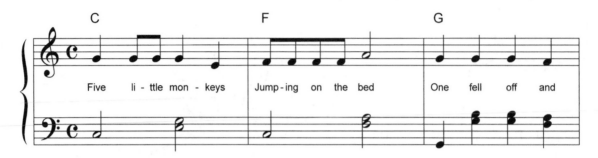

Five li - ttle mon - keys | Jump-ing on the bed | One fell off and

banged his head. | Sent for the do - ctor And the | do - ctor said

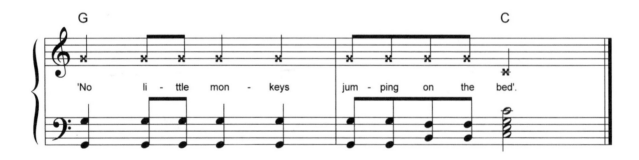

'No li - ttle mon - keys | jum - ping on the bed'.

Five Little Monkeys

(Five children in a row, raise shoulders and arms out and jump!)

Five little monkeys
Jumping on the bed
One fell off and banged his head.
(One child jumps out of the line.)

Sent for the doctor
And the doctor said 'No little monkeys jumping on the bed'.

(Four children in a row, raise shoulders and arms out and jump!)

Four little monkeys
Jumping on the bed
One fell off and banged his head.
(One child jumps out of the line.)

Sent for the doctor
And the doctor said 'No little monkeys jumping on the bed'.
(Three children in a row, raise shoulders and arms out and jump!)

Three little monkeys
Jumping on the bed
One fell off and banged his head.
(One child jumps out of the line.)

Sent for the doctor
And the doctor said 'No little monkeys jumping on the bed'.

(Two children in a row, raise shoulders and arms out and jump!)

Two little monkeys
Jumping on the bed
One fell off and banged his head.
(One child jumps out of the line.)

Sent for the doctor
And the doctor said 'No little monkeys jumping on the bed'.

(One child raises shoulders and arms out and jumps!)

One little monkey
Jumping on the bed
He fell off and banged his head.
Child jumps out of the line.

Sent for the doctor
And the doctor said 'No more monkeys jumping on the bed'.

Five Little Monkeys
How to use this song

Learning objectives

Stepping Stone
Show an interest in number problems.

Early Learning Goal
Find one more and one less than a number from one to 10. **(MD)**

Group size
Five children.

Sharing the song

Use this song to develop understanding of the concepts of subtraction and addition, safety, movement and planning a model, in themes such as 'Maths all around', 'Ourselves', 'Our bodies' and 'Toys'. Sing the song when a group of five children are on a clear, carpeted area, or outside or on a grassed or soft play area.

Introduce the song by giving each child a piece of white A4 paper on which is drawn an aerial view of a bed, inside a plastic wallet. Give everyone five small cards with a monkey drawn on each. Ask everyone to line up their monkeys on their beds. Play the song, asking everyone to join in and to remove one monkey at a time, according to the words.

Activity ideas

● Talk about why it is not safe to jump on a bed. Ask children to suggest places that would be safe, for example, a bouncy castle, trampoline, an open space. Let children build a model bouncy castle using small washing-up sponges and play people. **(PSED)**

● Say that, later on, one monkey with a headache decided to go back to bed followed, one at a time, by the rest. Ask everyone to join in with the rhyme below, using their bed pictures and monkey cards (see Sharing the song, above).

> One little monkey lying in bed
> He had an ache in his head
> One more came, and that made two.
> (and so on, up to five).
> Five little monkeys lying in bed
> All with an ache in their head!

(MD)

● Ask children to plan making a model of the jumping monkeys, suggesting which recycled materials they could use, and how they could make the model. For example, use a cereal packet for a bed, with five monkeys drawn on small pieces of card, each looped with wool onto a kitchen roll tube (see illustration). **(KUW)**

● Spread an old duvet cover (with a duvet inside, if possible), or an old blanket, on a carpeted area. Call this a bed and ask five children to be the monkeys. Think of other action words to substitute in the rhyme, such as hopping, crawling, rolling, rocking. **(PD)**